Coffee

(WAKE UP and BE GREAT!!!)

By: Quay Boddie

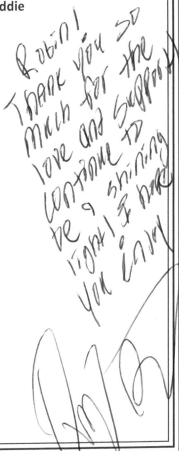

Robin!
Thank you so
much for the
love and support!
continue to
be a shining
light! I hope
you enjoy

Coffee (Wake UP and BE GREAT!!!) By
Quay Boddie

© 2018 Quay Boddie

Quay Boddie at *thaboddie@gmail.com*

ISBN-13: 978-1721652556

ISBN-10: 1721652558

Table of Contents

180 or 360?

Change in your life can be great! All

around change is a 360 because

maybe where you are right now, you

need a complete makeover. On the

flipside, maybe you just need to

switch some things; that's a 180.

Decide how much growth you want

and need!

Film Study

Being an athlete, you must watch

film to see what could be done better

as a player the next game. If you

don't study the performance then

how do you know what to correct?!

Think on this: Are you watching

everything that you do in hopes to

catch things that were wrong and

become a better player for life?

What do you do when you can't get the coffee right?

You know how you like for your

coffee to taste especially if you drink

it a lot! A little bit more of sugar or

cream and it just won't taste right at

all. In this moment, you can keep

drinking what you have or pour it out

and make a fresh cup. What I really

mean is: Your life will seem to be not

so great or unlikeable at times, but

YOU have all the ability and right to

either change it or feel sorry for

yourself and stay where you are. GET

YOUR COFFEE TOGETHER!!!

All In! (Invested)

It all depends on how much you put
into something! We get mad,
frustrated, and discouraged when
things don't go our way. First, we
must realize that we have to give our
all in all to see results and return on
our initial investment. Do you want
all God has to offer you; fully invest
in a relationship with him? Do you
want that business to be great; fully
invest yourself in it? WHATEVER you

want more of, have faith, invest, and

watch what happens. RETURNS WILL

COME!

Second Half

The game is not over with yet! Your

first half may have been ugly and full

of disappointment, but the second is

yours for the taking to win the game!

Hard spots are a part of the sport, but

always remember that you were

made to play! You can't and won't

lose! It's time to dig deep and finish

strong. Push, grind, press; REPEAT!

It's the second half! Let's get the

victory in our lives!!!

Impossible is POSSIBLE!

It's impossible if I don't try. It's

possible if I give it a shot. It's

impossible if I give into doubt. It's

possible if I become hungry. It's

impossible if I tell myself negative

things. It's possible if can just believe

and go forth! Drop the "I" and "M"

today because ALL things are

possible.

Taking NO'S but inheriting a YES

You ever get a letter from a school

and it said you were denied entrance

into a certain program? You ever get

a letter from an employer stating

that you didn't get the job you

applied for? You ever got dumped or

denied by that guy or girl that you

really loved? Ok ok by now you get

where I'm coming from right?! You

will take a lot of No's in your life, but

following the denials will always be acceptance from somewhere. You will have to experience rejection in this life at some points because it teaches you a lesson and it should remind you that something better always comes if the other things didn't work out.

Game plan (Life)

What's your strategy? If you don't

know it then figure it out. You must

first get a winning mindset, a will,

and determination! Let's start with

your offense, you must know how

you are going to score because

without points; you DON'T win.

Suggestion: Weapons of your offense

can include (Pushing yourself, having

faith, believing in yourself, going the

extra mile). Secondly, you must have

a defense to stop others from trying

to defeat you. Suggestion: Weapons

for your defense can include (Not

being distract from scoring, stop

what tries to stop you, never ever

give up because of what doubters

and haters have to say). Set your

game plan up to have a success in

this life. I'm not saying that you

won't lose at times or have setbacks,

but as long as you stay focused on

your principles and go with what you

know you will have great seasons and

many wins.

On the up and up!

Even when you are down; BE UP!

Who likes to be in the mud forever?!

You can get out of your mess before

you get out of your mess if you get

where I'm coming from! Have the "up

and up" attitude because with the

down you will stay down!

Get taught through anything

You can be taught a lesson at any

point of your life. For example, a

child will teach you to have patience

when dealing with them. Be aware

and pay attention to what happens in

your life because you don't want to

miss lessons that will help you along

the way.

Partial

The problem in the world is this: We live in a "half" society when we should be "full" in operation. Being partial in our relationships and marriages, partial on our jobs not giving 100 percent, partial in the church when doing the work of God. Partial, partial, partial and we have the nerve to complain about how things are going, but don't possess the will and want to make things

better!

Extreme measures

How far are you willing to go?

Sometimes you have to go far and

deep. You want to go to a place

where you have never been before?

Even your mindset must be different;

don't be like the rest! If you are an

artist, go to that radio station daily

and go all over to pass out your work;

somebody is going to eventually hear

you! If you are a ball player and want

to go to the next level, keep training

and trying out at different places; a

team will eventually pick you up.

Raising money for a good cause, keep

going at it until you meet your goal,

eventually you will have collected

more than enough funds. Extreme

measures are not for everyone, but

for those who will not settle for

crap!!!

Mentally

You have to be in tune with things in

order for them to work out! If your

mind isn't in it then you won't be

thinking clearly and most likely things

will be a disaster. Yes, make sure

your heart is in it, but don't ever

forget to just think.

Probably Never

Some will get on the band wagon and

support you for a while. Some

probably never will support you! In

either moment you have to not get

frustrated, but keep up with what

you are doing because at the end of

your day you might just have to go

and do things by yourself and learn to

be ok with it.

Giving up and letting go!

Giving up and letting go is equivalent

to your child on the ledge of a

building about to fall off and you let

them fall. You just can't do that; your

biggest victory is within you holding

on!

Coaches Clinic

All you have to do is run the play;

STICK TO THE PLAYBOOK! God is the

coach who gives you the playbook

(vision) and all you have to do is have

faith and run it!

C'mon man!

So do you really think that she is

going to just wait around for you?!

She supports you and loves you to

pieces, but you are going after what

you think is so great when you

already have great! Playing games is

for recess; give that girl what she

deserves.

Girl you crazy!

You holler all the time "It's not any

good men left." Then, you finally get

a good man, but you are so stuck on

the past crap that you let him slip

right through your fingers. Everybody

isn't out to hurt you or take

advantage of you! EASE UP and

RECOGNIZE when something real

enters your life!

Don't be my enemy

People will never take you serious if

you are always into with someone!

Want to be treated fairly, stop with

the senseless acts such as beefing,

competing with each other, and

arguing/bashing one another. We are

supposed to be united and as a team,

but we always divide ourselves

through our crazy actions.

Remember this...

#1 put your life in God's hands

#2 Live your life

Everything else will fall into place;

this I promise. It won't fall into place

unless you do it; that's key!

What's it gonna take?!

How many times will you take losses?

How many times will you allow

people to treat you like you are

nothing? How many times will you

not step up to the plate and do more

with yourself? Something will have to

give after while just know that!

Make it count

I remember playing baseball and

having a 3-2 count at the plate a lot

of times. I would be swinging away at

pitches; some not the best of pitches

just fouling them off. Finally my

coach would say "hang in there and

make it count!" The next pitch

thrown I would hit and find myself on

base. I said that to say this,

sometimes in life you will find

yourself swinging a lot in different

situations. Will you keep swinging no matter how hard or frustrating it gets so you can get on base (prosperous life) or will you allow yourself to strike out and give up when the count gets high? KEEP SWINGING!!!

What's your size?

No, I'm not referring to your physical

weight or height, but your mindset.

We end up tearing ourselves down

and also letting others do so. What

you have to realize is that you can be

as BIG or small as you want to be in

this life. Be a "Rock star" or be a

bum; it's your life and your choice.

*Spending time in your "closet"

What you talk to God about is very

personal. Yes, you have to get on a

personal level with Him in order for

Him to do great things for you. The

more we spend; the better! How

much time do you spend?

You got the juice

Point to yourself and say "I GOT THE
JUICE!" Is your tank feeling empty?
You have a lot of miles to go this
journey of life. There is always gas
that you know nothing about that
you must pull out and use when it's
time to! Those test, trials, and
hardships have NOTHING on you!
ENCOURAGE YOURSELF!

Cut differently

I have been through too much to

crumble anymore. Situations don't

define/describe me because they

don't rule over me! I have been

through the struggle, storm, and rain

and still I stand. Others faced

hardships and ended up losing

themselves in the process, but I

continue to hang in there! It's almost

like having a car that's plastic and a

car that's metal; the metal car will

last!

Feed for your soul

I can remember being in high school

and college F.C.A. (Fellowship of

Christian Athletes) and we would

always have good food to eat before

and after the meetings. Can you

believe that people would only come

to simply eat up the food and leave?!

Ooops I forgot to tell you, the

purpose of this organization in a

nutshell is to allow athletes to share

testimonies, talk about God, and

learn how to walk a good Christian walk. You had a lot of people that were so worried about feeding their faces instead of their souls! Feed your spirit and feed your soul because those are some things that you can hold on to will keep you together in your life. When you eat, make sure that you are eating of the right foods!

You don't have to take the bait!

Just because it's in your face doesn't

mean you have to cling to it. When

you know something is not good for

you why even entertain it? What's

going to happen is this, the thing that

you want so badly will turn around

and bite you in the tail. The girl or

guy may have a nice figure, but don't

let that mess up your relationship

with the one you go home to. Dirty

money may seem great because it's

so quick and easy to get, but don't let

it get you locked up! Do your best to

stay away from the hook!

They count you out

There was a high school baseball

team who had a great team and

made it to the playoffs every year.

The only problem was that the team

would lose in the first round EVERY

year. People talked about how bad

they were when playoff time would

come around and said these words

"they will NEVER make it to the next

round." Well, enough had become

enough. One season in particular the

team had made it to the next round

and "they" said "they just got lucky,

that team can't go any further." Well,

the team made it past the next round

and "they" said "they just got lucky,

there is no way they can keep

advancing." Fast forwarding, the

team ended up making it to the Final

Four that year; despite all of the

doubt, hate, and naysayers! I say all

that to say as long as you believe in

you and what you have going on you

will go as far as you want to go no

matter what "they" say. THEY don't

know what you have on the inside of

you to determine your future!

What does the bull do?

Ever been to a Rodeo before? There is a bull that is in a holding cell; hyped up and ready to get loose. In the cell if I had to guess, the bull is thinking "I'm about to have some fun and show out!" Check this out though: The bull is put into the cell to be prepped and also making him be patient until his time. Be like the bull!!! Right now, you may be in your holding cell, but you will have your time and turn to have fun and show

out too.

Tolerating trouble

As long as you live you will

experience trouble; that's just how it

is. Trouble will never go away no

matter if it's big or small trouble. 1 of

2 things can happen when dealing

with trouble. #1 you can let trouble

stress you to the max and take your

joy and peace or #2 you can learn

how to tolerate it and say I will push

pass this and maintain regardless.

YOU CAN DO IT!

Sometimes it's ok

I know it has been said not to look

back in your life, but I will say that

looking back is not always a bad thing

by far! You have to look back in the

right not the wrong way. Looking

back in the right way consist of

checking out the miracles, blessings,

and places you have experienced.

Looking back in the right way

reminds you that if great things have

been done for you before then they

are going to continue to happen as

long as you are on this side of the

earth.

What to do when in silence?

Do you ever feel like you are on

pause? Everything and everybody

around you is moving forward, but

you are stuck. Even though you may

feel this way, you know that things

are being worked out on your behalf

in the midst of it. Sometimes, you

may say to yourself "now, I know

that there has to be more to my life!"

Things may seem to be not working

for you right now, but stay

encouraged and know that you are

silenced because something major is

getting ready to happen. There is

some behind the scenes stuff

happening that you know nothing

about that is getting ready to blow

your mind!

How

How are things going to get done?

How am I going to pay my bills?

How am I going to fund my dreams

and goals?

We always ask "how," but remember

"how;" is not what we should worry

about. The "how" is in the hands of

someone who can fix all things, we

just have to keep on keeping on.

Dress it up!

You may not have a lot right now, but

nobody has to know it! Keep ironing

out the couple pair of jeans that you

do have until you get the jeans you

want. Keep cleaning and riding in

that car that you have right now until

you get a newer one; nobody has to

know that it's a crappy car. Keep on

eating potted meat and crackers until

you get to the steak and lobster etc

great is on the way, but for now just

make it look good.

Look around!

Take a couple of seconds and think of

everything you know that others

around you have done. Take a couple

of seconds to think about everything

that is attainable in this world. NOW,

IT'S YOUR TIME TO GO AND NOT

ONLY DO, BUT GO AND GET TOO!!!

Get with the program

People that say they love, care for

you, and want to be in your life have

to get with YOU and what you have

going on or get lost. Getting with the

program of your life requires a full

force and not a half way.

He cares

Babies cry for various reasons until they are comforted and have a sense of everything being ok. We cry out to God for various reasons now in our grown up lives and we end up being comforted! Translation: God will always hear our cry and always take care of us.

Something to

remember DAILY!

It's time for "worry" to pack its bags,

"Doubt" to walk out of the door,

"Fear" to go back to where it came

from!

Simple as that….

Lace em up

You can't play a field event without

cleats. Translation: You have to come

at life ready EVERYDAY! Lace up

those cleats and get ready to play.

Rain Rain

How long has it been raining in your life? Translation: How long have the trials and tribulations beat you down? Rain isn't a bad thing because it can wash away what seems to hold you down if you allow it to! If you can allow yourself to be worked on in the rain, when the sun comes out the blessings will too! You have to go through rain and pain to get the gain!!!

Let me remind you:

"Believing" has no start date! You can

start believing today and things will

change in your life.

Unbelief= No strength

Belief= STRENGTH FOREVER!

Fight to breathe, Fight to survive!

Be calm, be patient, figure things out,

but don't ever panic! Sometimes it

gets hot, hard to breathe, and heavy,

but keep telling yourself that YOU

WILL SURVIVE!

I'm not going home!

You will literally have to carry me out

before I lay down! I will fight, push

through, and press; no doubt! At the

end of the day, I know what I came

for and I know what I'm about! I have

come too far to take another route.

If you don't know, now you know!

When you don't know where the

resources you need are going to

come from; Jesus knows! Yes, the

test that come in your life seem to be

unbearable at times, but don't worry

because things are going to work out

on your behalf. If Jesus can take 5

loaves and 2 fish to feed 5,000 plus

then don't you think He is going to

work on your behalf for your little

problems??? Think about it...

Be Fair to "YOU"

Be fair to yourself! You deserve

everything that you can ever think or

dream of because of your hard work

and dedication to all you do. It may

not be appreciated by many, but

make sure you appreciate yourself.

Are you CONCRETE or Quicksand?

Concrete is hard to crack or move.

Quicksand moves with even the

slightest interruption. Translation:

When life throws curve balls at you

are you allowing them to break you

or are you letting them move you and

break your faith? We need CONCRETE

faith not quick and temporary faith.

Renew

Every chance you get make your

"renewal" count! A renewal is grace

and mercy that you receive on a daily

basis. No renew=No life

Keep saying that

We always say "I'll do it tomorrow,

next week, or whenever," but we are

hurting ourselves because before you

know it our lives will pass us by! Less

talking and more action!

Just start moving

One day you are going to get tired of

being left behind and start moving

because when you start moving you

can go a lot of places that you would

have never even imagined.

Fly Again

Trips can always happen for you

again and again. If you have the

ability to go once then you can again!

Translation: Success will come

around many times in your life.

#believeit

Rolling

KEEP UP YOUR MOMENTUM! Once

you stop rolling then it is hard to get

caught up. Events good and bad are

going to take place in your life, but

don't let it determine how you do

things; KEEP YOUR MOMENTUM!

When it's meant for you!

Just imagine you applying for a job

and just from talking on the phone to

a certain employer they already knew

that they wanted to hire you. You

come in for an interview with this

employer and the staff already knows

your name and things about you. You

don't even stay in the interview for

10 mins and you already have the

job. I say all this to say, what is

meant for you will always show up!

Step up to the plate!

Imagine if you were playing a sport

and your coach came and told you

that you would be starting in the

game right before game time. What

would you do? Are you going to be

prepared at all times?

Fall in love with the rain!

We look at the rain as being (yucky,

nasty, and unbearable) at times and

we don't even want to go into it. Not

even thinking, we grow in the rain

because we learn to become better

and stronger in it. Yes, there is pain,

but if you stay faithful even in the

uncomfortable spots you will see that

the rain actually symbolizes the

abundance, overflow, and blessings

that are falling on your life.

Pebbles

Pebbles are just pebbles;

Translation:

Don't let the small stuff stop you!

Flame

Just because they don't see or don't

acknowledge your flame doesn't

mean that you aren't hot! You turn

up the heat by yourself and let

everybody else feel it later.

Home is first!

You can't expect to get to the nations

if you don't take care of what's at

home first. Translation: Yes, we want

to go and do so much more, but if we

don't take care of what's in our grasp

right now then how can we handle a

big load?

Acknowledge God!

Funny, but true…think about when

you are in a rush to get to the

bathroom. When you finally get

there, what is the first thing that you

say? "Thank you Lord!" We shouldn't

only acknowledge God when we are

just in a crisis, we should

acknowledge Him In all things!!!

There are no limits!

We get stuck in the hallway (limited)

when there is a door we can walk

through to the outside (unlimited).

We have to step outside of the norm!

Condition it!

It's almost training a dog, baby, or whatever; you have to condition it! Eventually, if you keep on giving attention to it then something great will come from it. Translation: You have been sowing, sowing, and sowing so now you are bound to reap something so major that it will be worth the wait of your long journey!

Can you hear?

Are you dealing with a lot of static in

your life? We have to make sure that

we are on the right station (listening

to the right things in our lives)

Getting on the right station makes

everything else flow so much

smoother for us.

Sell out!

You can't have the half packed arena

mindset; you must have the "sold

out" mentality! You want something

then go figure out to obtain it!

You ever been to the beach before?

You will see waves: some big and some small. Waves constantly move due to things such as wind and other components of nature.

What am I getting at?

-When the wind and water seem to get out of control because it will; don't waver in your faith! Become a still body of water!

Laundry Terms

Everything is all "folded" up right now because there is a specific day/time that you wear something. I know that it seems like you are running out of things to put on, but today put on your best faith, trust, and belief that you have and know that God is going to unfold some fresh and if not new clothes for you!!!

Check the mail

Some good mail is coming your way soon and very soon! We sometimes check the mailbox to find a bunch of junk mail, coupons, etc. Bad news, unwanted news, crazy news is coming to an end for you. Watch out for your delivery of better and greater because it is overdue for you to receive what you have been waiting on.

And now what?!

There are times in your life where your faith will be tested and it seems that God is nowhere near you. At this time, the devil/enemy is in your ear saying "and now what are you going to do???"

Your reply: I am going to do what I have always done! TRUST GOD!